300 FOOTBALL Quizzes

Test Your Knowledge on The Beautiful Game

This Book Belongs to:

_____

Contents

World Cup

Q1: When was the first FIFA World Cup held?

a) 1926

b) 1930

c) 1940

Q2: Which country hosted the first World Cup?

a) Italy

b) Uruguay

c) England

Q3: Who won the first FIFA World Cup in 1930?

a) Argentina

b) Brazil

c) Uruguay

Q4: How many teams participate in the FIFA World Cup?

a) 16 teams

b) 24 teams

c) 32 teams

Q5: How often is the FIFA World Cup held?

a) Every two years

b) Every three years

c) Every four years

Q6: Which country has won the most World Cups?

a) Italy

b) Brazil

c) Germany

Q7: Who won the World Cup 2022?

a) France

b) Argentina

c) Brazil

Q8: Which country hosted the World Cup 2022?

a) Russia

b) Qatar

c) United Arab Emirates

Q9: When did the World Cup 2022 take place and why was it different from previous editions?

a) May to June; To avoid conflicts with other events

b) November to December; To avoid extreme heat in the host nation

c) July to August; To align with traditional summer scheduling

Q10: Who is the best player in the World Cup 2022?

a) Cristiano Ronaldo

b) Lionel Messi

c) Neymar Jr.

Q11: Which country became the first African nation to reach the semi-finals of the World Cup?

a) Ghana

b) Nigeria

c) Morocco

Q12: How did Croatia perform in the World Cup and what was their achievement?

a) Quarter-finals; First-time appearance

b) Semi-finals; Second consecutive appearance

c) Round of 16; Debut appearance

Q13: Who is the all-time leading scorer in World Cup history?

a) Ronaldo Nazário

b) Pelé

c) Miroslav Klose

Q14: Which country won the 2018 FIFA World Cup?

a) France

b) Germany

c) Brazil

Q15: What is the official trophy awarded to the World Cup winners called?

a) World Cup Trophy

b) FIFA Trophy

c) Jules Rimet Trophy

Q16: Which country has hosted the most World Cups?

a) Brazil

b) Germany

c) Italy

Q17: Which country won the World Cup three times in a row?

a) Italy

b) Brazil

c) Germany

Q18: Who is the youngest player to score a goal in World Cup history?

a) Lionel Messi

b) Kylian Mbappé

c) Pelé

Q19: Which country won the World Cup in 1966?

a) Brazil

b) England

c) Italy

Q20: Who scored the "Hand of God" goal in the 1986 World Cup?

a) Diego Maradona

b) Pelé

c) Johan Cruyff

Q21: Which country hosted the 2014 FIFA World Cup?

a) Brazil

b) Germany

c) Spain

Q22: Who is the all-time leading assist provider in World Cup history?

a) Lionel Messi

b) Cristiano Ronaldo

c) Thomas Müller from Germany

Q23: Who is the coach with the most World Cup wins?

a) Joachim Löw from Germany

b) Vittorio Pozzo from Italy

c) Diego Maradona from Argentina

Q24: Which country won the World Cup in 1954?

a) Italy

b) Brazil

c) West Germany

Q25: Who scored the fastest goal in World Cup history?

a) Cristiano Ronaldo

b) Hakan Şükür from Turkey

c) Lionel Messi

Q26: Which country won the World Cup in 1978?

a) Brazil

b) Argentina

c) Italy

Q27: Who is the player with the most World Cup appearances?

a) Lothar Matthäus from Germany

b) Pelé from Brazil

c) Diego Maradona from Argentina

Q28: Which country has reached the most World Cup finals without winning?

a) Brazil

b) Germany

c) The Netherlands

Q29: Who scored the winning goal in the 2010 World Cup final?

a) Cristiano Ronaldo

b) Lionel Messi

c) Andrés Iniesta from Spain

Q30: Which country won the World Cup in 1958?

a) France

b) Brazil

c) Italy

Q31: Who is the oldest player to play in a World Cup match?

a) Essam El-Hadary from Egypt

b) Gianluigi Buffon from Italy

c) David Beckham from England

Q32: Which country won the World Cup in 1994?

A: Brazil

B: Italy

C: Germany

Q33: Who won the Golden Ball award in the 2018 World Cup?

A: Luka Modrić from Croatia

B: Lionel Messi from Argentina

C: Cristiano Ronaldo from Portugal

Q34: Which country won the World Cup in 1962?

A: Brazil

B: Germany

C: Argentina

Q35: Who is the goalkeeper with the most clean sheets in World Cup history?

A: Dino Zoff from Italy

B: Manuel Neuer from Germany

C: Lev Yashin from Russia

Q36: Which country won the World Cup in 1982?

A: Italy

B: Brazil

C: France

Q37: Which country won the World Cup in 1974?

A: West Germany

B: Argentina

C: Brazil

Q38: Who scored the most goals in a single World Cup tournament?

A: Just Fontaine from France

B: Pelé from Brazil

C: Diego Maradona from Argentina

Q39: Which country won the World Cup in 2006?

A: Italy

B: Spain

C: France

Q40: Who won the Golden Boot award in the 2014 World Cup?

A: James Rodríguez from Colombia

B: Thomas Müller from Germany

C: Neymar Jr. from Brazil

Q41: Which country won the World Cup in 2010?

A: Spain

B: Germany

C: Brazil

Q42: Who won the Golden Ball award in the 2014 World Cup?

A: Lionel Messi from Argentina

B: Cristiano Ronaldo from Portugal

C: Neymar Jr. from Brazil

Q43: Which country won the World Cup in 2002?

A: Brazil

B: Italy

C: Germany

Q44: Who won the Golden Boot award in the 2010 World Cup?

A: Thomas Müller from Germany

B: David Villa from Spain

C: Wesley Sneijder from Netherlands

Q45: Which country won the World Cup in 1998?

A: France

B: Brazil

C: Italy

Q46: Who won the Golden Ball award in the 2010 World Cup?

A: Diego Forlán from Uruguay

B: Xavi from Spain

C: Andrés Iniesta from Spain

Q47: Which country won the World Cup in 1986?

A: Argentina

B: Brazil

C: Italy

Q48: Who won the Golden Boot award in the 2006 World Cup?

A: Miroslav Klose from Germany

B: Thierry Henry from France

C: Luca Toni from Italy

Q49: Which country won the World Cup in 1982?

A: Italy

B: Brazil

C: Germany

Q50: Who won the Golden Ball award in the 2006 World Cup?

A: Zinedine Zidane from France

B: Fabio Cannavaro from Italy

C: Ronaldinho from Brazil

Answers

Q1: When was the first FIFA World Cup held?

b) 1930

Q2: Which country hosted the first World Cup?

b) Uruguay

Q3: Who won the first FIFA World Cup in 1930?

c) Uruguay

Q4: How many teams participate in the FIFA World Cup?

c) 32 teams

Q5: How often is the FIFA World Cup held?

c) Every four years

Q6: Which country has won the most World Cups?

b) Brazil

Q7: Who won the World Cup 2022?

b) Argentina

Q8: Which country hosted the World Cup 2022?

b) Qatar

Q9: When did the World Cup 2022 take place and why was it different from previous editions?

b) November to December; To avoid extreme heat in the host nation

Q10: Who is the best player in the World Cup 2022?

b) Lionel Messi

Q11: Which country became the first African nation to reach the semi-finals of the World Cup?

c) Morocco

Q12: How did Croatia perform in the World Cup and what was their achievement?

b) Semi-finals; Second consecutive appearance

Q13: Who is the all-time leading scorer in World Cup history?

c) Miroslav Klose

Q14: Which country won the 2018 FIFA World Cup?

a) France

Q15: What is the official trophy awarded to the World Cup winners called?

a) World Cup Trophy

Q16: Which country has hosted the most World Cups?

a) Brazil

Q17: Which country won the World Cup three times in a row?

a) Italy

Q18: Who is the youngest player to score a goal in World Cup history?

c) Pelé

Q19: Which country won the World Cup in 1966?

b) England

Q20: Who scored the "Hand of God" goal in the 1986 World Cup?

a) Diego Maradona

Q21: Which country hosted the 2014 FIFA World Cup?

a) Brazil

Q22: Who is the all-time leading assist provider in World Cup history?

c) Thomas Müller from Germany

Q23: Who is the coach with the most World Cup wins?

b) Vittorio Pozzo from Italy

Q24: Which country won the World Cup in 1954?

c) West Germany

Q25: Who scored the fastest goal in World Cup history?

b) Hakan Şükür from Turkey

Q26: Which country won the World Cup in 1978?

b) Argentina

Q27: Who is the player with the most World Cup appearances?

a) Lothar Matthäus from Germany

Q28: Which country has reached the most World Cup finals without winning?

c) The Netherlands

Q29: Who scored the winning goal in the 2010 World Cup final?

c) Andrés Iniesta from Spain

Q30: Which country won the World Cup in 1958?

b) Brazil

Q31: Who is the oldest player to play in a World Cup match?

a) Essam El-Hadary from Egypt

Q32: Which country won the World Cup in 1994?

a) Brazil

Q33: Who won the Golden Ball award in the 2018 World Cup?

b) Luka Modrić from Croatia

Q34: Which country won the World Cup in 1962?

a) Brazil

Q35:Who is the goalkeeper with the most clean sheets in World Cup history?

b) Dino Zoff from Italy

Q36: Which country won the World Cup in 1982?

b) Italy

Q37: Which country won the World Cup in 1974?

b) West Germany

Q38: Who scored the most goals in a single World Cup tournament?

a) Just Fontaine from France

Q39: Which country won the World Cup in 2006?

b) Italy

Q40: Who won the Golden Boot award in the 2014 World Cup?

a) James Rodríguez from Colombia

Q41: Which country won the World Cup in 2010?

b) Spain

Q42: Who won the Golden Ball award in the 2014 World Cup?

b) Lionel Messi from Argentina

Q43: Which country won the World Cup in 2002?

a) Brazil

Q44: Who won the Golden Boot award in the 2010 World Cup?

a) Thomas Müller from Germany

Q45: Which country won the World Cup in 1998?

a) France

Q46: Who won the Golden Ball award in the 2010 World Cup?

b) Diego Forlán from Uruguay

Q47: Which country won the World Cup in 1986?

a) Argentina

Q48: Who won the Golden Boot award in the 2006 World Cup?

a) Miroslav Klose from Germany

Q49: Which country won the World Cup in 1982?

b) Italy

Q50: Who won the Golden Ball award in the 2006 World Cup?

b) Zinedine Zidane from France

Euro

Q1: How was the Euro Cup (2020) tournament of that year unique in

terms of hosting?

a) It was hosted by a single country.

b) It was hosted by multiple countries.

c) It was played in a neutral venue.

Q2: How many teams were part of the Euro Cup (2020)?

a) 12 teams

b) 16 teams

c) 24 teams

Q3: How did the teams advance to the next phase of the tournament?

a) Top two teams from each group advance.

b) Bottom two teams from each group advance.

c) A random draw determines the advancing teams.

Q4: Where was the final of the Euro Cup (2020) held and which teams

played in it?

a) Final was held in Rome; Italy vs. Germany

b) Final was held in London; Italy vs. England

c) Final was held in Paris; France vs. Portugal

Q5: Which team won the final of the Euro Cup (2020), and how was the victory achieved?

a) England, won in extra time

b) Italy, won on penalties

c) Portugal, won in regular time

Q6: Who emerged as the top scorer of the Euro Cup (2020)?

a) Cristiano Ronaldo

b) Kylian Mbappé

c) Harry Kane

Q7: Who were the recipients of the Golden Boot award for the Euro Cup (2020)?

a) Cristiano Ronaldo and Antoine Griezmann

b) Robert Lewandowski and Romelu Lukaku

c) Cristiano Ronaldo and Patrik Schick

Q8: Who was recognized as the best player of the Euro Cup (2020)?

a) Harry Kane

b) Luka Modrić

c) Gianluigi Donnarumma

Q9: What notable achievements contributed to Gianluigi Donnarumma being awarded the best player of the tournament?

a) Scoring the most goals in the tournament

b) Making crucial saves and winning the Golden Glove

c) Captaining his team to victory

Q10: Who was honored as the best young player of the tournament?

a) João Cancelo

b) Pedri

c) Phil Foden

Q11: When was the first UEFA European Championship held?

a) 1956

b) 1960

c) 1964

Q12: How often is the Euro Cup held?

a) Every two years

b) Every four years

c) Every six years

Q13: Which country has won the most Euro Cup titles?

a) Italy

b) Germany

c) Spain

Q14: Who is the all-time leading scorer in the Euro Cup?

a) Thierry Henry

b) Michel Platini

c) Cristiano Ronaldo

Q15: Who scored the most goals in a single Euro Cup tournament?

a) Cristiano Ronaldo

b) Antoine Griezmann

c) Michel Platini

Q16: Which country holds the record for the highest number of goals in a single Euro Cup tournament?

a) France

b) Germany

c) Spain

Q17: Who is the manager with the most Euro Cup titles?

a) Vicente del Bosque

b) Joachim Löw

c) Didier Deschamps

Q18: Which country won the first-ever Euro Cup?

a) West Germany

b) France

c) Soviet Union

Q19: Who is the youngest player to score in a Euro Cup tournament?

a) Michael Owen

b) Wayne Rooney

c) Johan Vonlanthen

Q20: Which country has reached the most Euro Cup finals without winning the title?

a) Belgium

b) Netherlands

c) Portugal

Q21: Who scored the fastest goal in a Euro Cup match?

a) Dmitri Kirichenko

b) Lukas Podolski

c) Zlatan Ibrahimović

Q22: Which country holds the record for the longest unbeaten streak in Euro Cup matches?

a) Spain

b) Germany

c) Italy

Q23: Who scored the most goals in total Euro Cup tournaments?

a) Cristiano Ronaldo

b) Michel Platini

c) Thierry Henry

Q24: Which country holds the record for the most consecutive Euro Cup titles?

a) Spain

b) Germany

Q25: Who is the player with the most appearances in Euro Cup matches?

a) Cristiano Ronaldo

b) Xavi

c) Andrea Pirlo

Q26: Which country holds the record for the most goals scored in Euro Cup history?

a) Germany

b) France

c) Spain

Q27: Which country has the most appearances in the Euro Cup finals without winning the title?

a) Germany

b) Netherlands

c) Portugal

Q28: Which country holds the record for the most consecutive Euro Cup semifinal appearances?

a) Germany

b) Spain

c) France

Q29: Which country has the most appearances in the Euro Cup semifinals?

a) Germany

b) France

c) Italy

Q30: Which country holds the record for the most consecutive Euro Cup group stage victories?

a) Spain

b) Germany

c) Belgium

Q31: Which country has the most Euro Cup participation without winning the title?

a) England

b) Belgium

c) Scotland

Q32: Which country has the most Euro Cup participation without reaching the semifinals?

a) Romania

b) Turkey

c) Wales

Q33: Which country holds the record for the most Euro Cup group-stage victories?

a) Spain

b) Germany

c) Italy

Q34: Who scored the first goal in Euro Cup history?

a) Viktor Ponedelnik

b) Ferenc Puskás

c) Helmut Rahn

Q35: Which country has scored the most goals in a single Euro Cup match?

a) France

b) Spain

c) Netherlands

Q36: Which country has the most Euro Cup appearances without reaching the final?

a) England

b) Belgium

c) Portugal

Q37: Who is the player with the most assists in Euro Cup history?

a) Luís Figo

b) Cristiano Ronaldo

c) Xavi

Q38: Which country has reached the most Euro Cup finals without winning the title?

a) Netherlands

b) Germany

c) Portugal

Answers

Q1: How was the Euro Cup (2020) tournament of that year unique in terms of hosting?

b) It was hosted by multiple countries.

Q2: How many teams were part of the Euro Cup (2020)?

c) 24 teams

Q3: How did the teams advance to the next phase of the tournament?

a) Top two teams from each group advance.

Q4: Where was the final of the Euro Cup (2020) held and which teams played in it?

b) Final was held in London; Italy vs. England

Q5: Which team won the final of the Euro Cup (2020), and how was the victory achieved?

b) Italy, won on penalties

Q6: Who emerged as the top scorer of the Euro Cup (2020)?

a) Cristiano Ronaldo

Q7: Who were the recipients of the Golden Boot award for the Euro Cup (2020)?

c) Cristiano Ronaldo and Patrik Schick

Q8: Who was recognized as the best player of the Euro Cup (2020)?

c) Gianluigi Donnarumma

Q9: What notable achievements contributed to Gianluigi Donnarumma being awarded the best player of the tournament?

b) Making crucial saves and winning the Golden Glove

Q10: Who was honored as the best young player of the tournament?

b) Pedri

Q11: When was the first UEFA European Championship held?

b) 1960

Q12: How often is the Euro Cup held?

b) Every four years

Q13: Which country has won the most Euro Cup titles?

c) Spain

Q14: Who is the all-time leading scorer in the Euro Cup?

b) Michel Platini

Q15: Who scored the most goals in a single Euro Cup tournament?

c) Michel Platini

Q16: Which country holds the record for the highest number of goals in a single Euro Cup tournament?

A: a) France

Q17: Who is the manager with the most Euro Cup titles?

a) Vicente del Bosque

Q18: Which country won the first-ever Euro Cup?

c) Soviet Union

Q19: Who is the youngest player to score in a Euro Cup tournament?

c) Johan Vonlanthen

Q20: Which country has reached the most Euro Cup finals without winning the title?

b) Netherlands

Q21: Who scored the fastest goal in a Euro Cup match?

a) Dmitri Kirichenko

Q22: Which country holds the record for the longest unbeaten streak in Euro Cup matches?

a) Spain

Q23: Who scored the most goals in total Euro Cup tournaments?

a) Cristiano Ronaldo

Q24: Which country holds the record for the most consecutive Euro Cup titles?

a) Spain

Q25: Who is the player with the most appearances in Euro Cup matches?

a) Cristiano Ronaldo

Q26: Which country holds the record for the most goals scored in Euro Cup history?

a) Germany

Q27: Which country has the most appearances in the Euro Cup finals without winning the title?

a) Germany

Q28: Which country holds the record for the most consecutive Euro Cup semifinal appearances?

a) Germany

Q29: Which country has the most appearances in the Euro Cup semifinals?

a) Germany

Q30: Which country holds the record for the most consecutive Euro Cup group stage victories?

a) Spain

Q31: Which country has the most Euro Cup participation without winning the title?

a) England

Q32: Which country has the most Euro Cup participation without reaching the semifinals?

a) Romania

Q33: Which country holds the record for the most Euro Cup group-stage victories?

a) Spain

Q34: Who scored the first goal in Euro Cup history?

a) Viktor Ponedelnik

Q35: Which country has scored the most goals in a single Euro Cup match?

a) France

Q36: Which country has the most Euro Cup appearances without reaching the final?

a) England

Q37: Who is the player with the most assists in Euro Cup history?

a) Luís Figo

Q38: Which country has reached the most Euro Cup finals without winning the title?

a) Netherlands

Premier League

Q1: Who was the champion of the Premier League in the 2022/23 season?

a) Manchester United

b) Liverpool

c) Manchester City

Q2: Who clinched the top scorer title in the Premier League for the 2022/23 season?

a) Cristiano Ronaldo

b) Mohamed Salah

c) Erling Haaland

Q3: Who stood out as the player with the most assists in the Premier League during the 2022/23 season?

a) Bruno Fernandes

b) Kevin De Bruyne

c) Jack Grealish

Q4: Who won the Premier League Manager of the Season award in the 2022/23 season?

a) Jürgen Klopp

b) Pep Guardiola

c) Ole Gunnar Solskjær

Q5: When was the English Premier League founded?

a) 1980

b) 1992

c) 2000

Q6: How many teams participate in the Premier League?

a) 18

b) 20

c) 22

Q7: Which team has won the most Premier League titles?

a) Liverpool

b) Chelsea

c) Manchester United

Q8: Who is the all-time leading scorer in the Premier League?

a) Thierry Henry

b) Alan Shearer

c) Wayne Rooney

Q9: Which team won the inaugural Premier League season in 1992-1993?

a) Manchester City

b) Arsenal

c) Manchester United

Q10: Who is the manager with the most Premier League titles?

a) José Mourinho

b) Arsène Wenger

c) Sir Alex Ferguson

Q11: Which stadium has the highest capacity in the Premier League?

a) Anfield

b) Old Trafford

c) Emirates Stadium

Q12: Who won the Golden Boot award in the 2020-2021 Premier League season?

a) Jamie Vardy

b) Mohamed Salah

c) Harry Kane

Q13: Which team has the most consecutive Premier League titles?

a) Manchester United

b) Chelsea

c) Arsenal

Q14: Who has won the most Premier League Manager of the Season awards?

a) José Mourinho

b) Sir Alex Ferguson

c) Pep Guardiola

Q15: Who has the record for the most assists in a single Premier League season?

a) Cesc Fàbregas

b) Kevin De Bruyne

c) Thierry Henry

Q16: Which player has won the most Premier League Player of the Month awards?

a) Harry Kane

b) Cristiano Ronaldo

c) Steven Gerrard

Q17: Which team has the longest unbeaten streak in the Premier League?

a) Manchester City

b) Arsenal

c) Liverpool

Q18: Who won the Premier League title in the 2019-2020 season?

a) Chelsea

b) Manchester City

c) Liverpool

Q19: Who is the player with the most Premier League appearances?

a) John Terry

b) Ryan Giggs

c) Gareth Barry

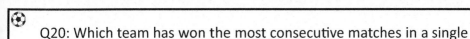

Q20: Which team has won the most consecutive matches in a single

Premier League season?

a) Liverpool

b) Manchester City

c) Manchester United

Q21: Who is the oldest player to score in the Premier League?

a) Ryan Giggs

b) Teddy Sheringham

c) Frank Lampard

Q22: Which team has the most goals in a single Premier League season?

a) Manchester City

b) Liverpool

c) Manchester United

Q23: Who won the Premier League title in the 2018-2019 season?

a) Manchester United

b) Manchester City

c) Liverpool

Q24: Which player has won the most Premier League Golden Glove

awards?

a) Petr Čech and Alisson Becker

b) David De Gea

c) Thibaut Courtois

Q25: Who is the highest-scoring defender in Premier League history?

a) John Terry

b) Rio Ferdinand

c) Nemanja Vidić

Q26: Which team has won the most Premier League titles consecutively?

a) Manchester United

b) Chelsea

c) Manchester United and Chelsea

Q27: Who won the Premier League title in the 2017-2018 season?

a) Manchester United

b) Manchester City

c) Liverpool

Q28: Who is the player with the most assists in Premier League history?

a) Frank Lampard

b) Steven Gerrard

c) Ryan Giggs

Q29: Who has won the most Premier League Manager of the Month awards?

a) Sir Alex Ferguson

b) José Mourinho

c) Arsène Wenger

Q30: Which team has the most points in a single Premier League season?

a) Manchester City

b) Liverpool

c) Manchester United

Q31: Who won the Premier League title in the 2016-2017 season?

a) Manchester United

b) Chelsea

c) Manchester City

Q32: Who has scored the fastest goal in Premier League history?

a) Alan Shearer

b) Wayne Rooney

c) Shane Long

Q33: Which team has the most consecutive seasons in the Premier League?

a) Arsenal

b) Manchester United

c) Liverpool

Q34: Who won the Premier League title in the 2015-2016 season?

a) Arsenal

b) Manchester City

c) Leicester City

Q35: Who has won the most Premier League Golden Boot awards?

a) Thierry Henry

b) Cristiano Ronaldo

c) Alan Shearer

Q36: Who scored the most goals in a single Premier League season?

a) Alan Shearer

b) Andy Cole

c) Alan Shearer and Andy Cole

Q37: Who won the Premier League title in the 2014-2015 season?

a) Manchester United

b) Chelsea

c) Manchester City

Q38: Who is the youngest player to captain a team in the Premier League?

a) Jack Wilshere

b) Wayne Rooney

c) Steven Gerrard

Q39: Which team has won the fewest points in a single Premier League season?

a) Derby County

b) Sunderland

c) Norwich City

Q40: Who won the Premier League title in the 2013-2014 season?

a) Manchester City

b) Liverpool FC

c) Chelsea FC

Q41: Who is the oldest player to debut in the Premier League?

a) Mark Schwarzer

b) Brad Friedel

c) Tim Howard

Q42: Which team has the most goals in Premier League history?

a) Manchester United

b) Liverpool FC

c) Arsenal FC

Q43: Who won the Premier League title in the 2012-2013 season?

a) Manchester City

b) Manchester United

c) Chelsea FC

Q44: Who is the player with the most assists in a single Premier League season?

a) Kevin De Bruyne

b) Thierry Henry

c) Mesut Özil

Q45: Who is the all-time leading scorer in the Premier League?

a) Wayne Rooney

b) Thierry Henry

c) Alan Shearer

Q46: Which club is known as the "Invincibles" after an unbeaten season?

a) Arsenal FC

b) Manchester United

c) Chelsea FC

Q47: Who holds the record for the most consecutive Premier League appearances?

a) Brad Friedel

b) Gareth Barry

c) Frank Lampard

Q48: Which Premier League team has the most consecutive wins in a single season?

a) Manchester City

b) Liverpool FC

c) Chelsea FC

Q49: Which player is often referred to as "Captain Fantastic" and played for Liverpool?

a) Steven Gerrard

b) Frank Lampard

c) Roy Keane

Q50: Who is the youngest player to score a Premier League goal?

a) James Vaughan

b) Wayne Rooney

c) Raheem Sterling

Q51: Which Premier League club is known for its "You'll Never Walk Alone" anthem?

a) Liverpool FC

b) Manchester United

c) Arsenal FC

Q52: Which stadium has the record attendance for a Premier League match?

a) Old Trafford

b) Anfield

c) Wembley Stadium

Q53: Who is the player with the most Premier League appearances?

a) Gareth Barry

b) Frank Lampard

c) Ryan Giggs

Q54: Which team won the Premier League title in the 2015/16 season against all odds?

a) Leicester City

b) Chelsea FC

c) Manchester City

Q55: Who is known as "The Special One" and has managed several Premier League clubs?

a) José Mourinho

b) Sir Alex Ferguson

c) Arsène Wenger

Q56: Which Premier League club is often referred to as "The Red Devils"?

a) Manchester United

b) Liverpool FC

c) Chelsea FC

Q57: Which club's supporters are known as "The Kop"?

a) Liverpool FC

b) Manchester United

c) Tottenham Hotspur

Q58: Who won the Premier League title in the 2019/20 season?

a) Liverpool FC

b) Manchester City

c) Chelsea FC

Q59: Which club has the nickname "The Gunners"?

a) Arsenal FC

b) Manchester United

c) Tottenham Hotspur

Q60: Who holds the record for the most goals scored in a single Premier League season?

a) Alan Shearer

b) Andy Cole

c) Thierry Henry

Q61: Which team has won the most consecutive Premier League titles?

a) Manchester United

b) Chelsea

c) Both a and b

Q62: Who is the youngest player to make a Premier League appearance?

a) Harvey Elliott

b) James Milner

c) Phil Foden

Q63: Which club's supporters are known as "The Citizens"?

a) Manchester City FC

b) Chelsea FC

c) Liverpool FC

Q64: Who holds the record for the most consecutive Premier League clean sheets?

a) Petr Čech

b) Alisson Becker

c) Ederson

Q65: Which club's supporters are known as "The Blues"?

a) Chelsea FC

b) Everton FC

c) Manchester City FC

Q66: Which club's supporters are known as "The Spurs"?

a) Tottenham Hotspur FC

b) Arsenal FC

c) West Ham United FC

Q67: Who holds the record for the most Premier League goals in a calendar year?

a) Harry Kane

b) Alan Shearer

c) Thierry Henry

Q68: Who is the player with the most goals scored as a substitute in Premier League history?

a) Jermain Defoe

b) Ole Gunnar Solskjær

c) Nwankwo Kanu

Q69: Which club's supporters are known as "The Toffees"?

a) Everton FC

b) Newcastle United FC

c) Burnley FC

Q70: Who is the player with the most red cards in Premier League history?

a) Richard Dunne

b) Patrick Vieira

c) Roy Keane

Q71: Which club's supporters are known as "The Clarets"?

a) Burnley FC

b) Aston Villa FC

c) Crystal Palace FC

Q72: Who is the player with the most own goals in Premier League history?

a) Richard Dunne

b) Jamie Carragher

c) Wes Brown

Q73: Which club's supporters are known as "The Canaries"?

a) Norwich City FC

b) West Ham United FC

c) Swansea City FC

Q74: Who is the player with the most Premier League appearances as a goalkeeper?

a) Petr Čech

b) Brad Friedel

c) David James

Q75: Which team holds the record for the most consecutive away wins in the Premier League?

a) Chelsea FC

b) Manchester City FC

c) Liverpool FC

Q76: Which club's supporters are known as "The Hornets"?

a) Watford FC

b) Bournemouth FC

c) Brighton & Hove Albion FC

Q77: Who is the player with the most Premier League hat-tricks?

a) Alan Shearer

b) Thierry Henry

c) Sergio Agüero

Q78: Which team holds the record for the most consecutive Premier League draws?

a) Derby County

b) Aston Villa FC

c) Southampton FC

Q79: Which club's supporters are known as "The Baggies"?

a) West Bromwich Albion FC

b) Sunderland AFC

c) Fulham FC

Q80: Which club's supporters are known as "The Saints"?

a) Southampton FC

b) Crystal Palace FC

c) Wolverhampton Wanderers FC

Q81: Which club's supporters are known as "The Eagles"?

a) Crystal Palace FC

b) Aston Villa FC

Answers

Q1: Who was the champion of the Premier League in the 2022/23 season?

a) Manchester City

Q2: Who clinched the top scorer title in the Premier League for the 2022/23 season?

a) Erling Haaland

Q3: Who stood out as the player with the most assists in the Premier League during the 2022/23 season?

a) Kevin De Bruyne

Q4: Who won the Premier League Manager of the Season award in the 2022/23 season?

a) Pep Guardiola

Q5: When was the English Premier League founded?

b) 1992

Q6: How many teams participate in the Premier League?

b) 20 teams

Q7: Which team has won the most Premier League titles?

a) Manchester United

Q8: Who is the all-time leading scorer in the Premier League?

c) Alan Shearer

Q9: Which team won the inaugural Premier League season in 1992-1993?

a) Manchester United

Q10: Who is the manager with the most Premier League titles?

c) Sir Alex Ferguson

Q11: Which stadium has the highest capacity in the Premier League?

c) Old Trafford

Q12: Who won the Golden Boot award in the 2020-2021 Premier League season?

b) Mohamed Salah

Q13: Which team has the most consecutive Premier League titles?

c) Manchester United

Q14: Who has won the most Premier League Manager of the Season awards?

c) Sir Alex Ferguson

Q15: Who has the record for the most assists in a single Premier League season?

a) Kevin De Bruyne

Q16: Which player has won the most Premier League Player of the Month awards?

b) Steven Gerrard

Q17: Which team has the longest unbeaten streak in the Premier League?

b) Arsenal

Q18: Who won the Premier League title in the 2019-2020 season?

c) Liverpool

Q19: Who is the player with the most Premier League appearances?

c) Gareth Barry

Q20: Which team has won the most consecutive matches in a single Premier League season?

a) Manchester City

Q21: Who is the oldest player to score in the Premier League?

a) Teddy Sheringham

Q22: Which team has the most goals in a single Premier League season?

b) Manchester City

Q23: Who won the Premier League title in the 2018-2019 season?

c) Manchester City

Q24: Which player has won the most Premier League Golden Glove awards?

a) Petr Čech

Q25: Who is the highest-scoring defender in Premier League history?

a) John Terry

Q26: Which team has won the most Premier League titles consecutively?

c) Chelsea

Q27: Who won the Premier League title in the 2017-2018 season?

a) Manchester City

Q28: Who is the player with the most assists in Premier League history?

a) Ryan Giggs

Q29: Who has won the most Premier League Manager of the Month awards?

a) Sir Alex Ferguson

Q30: Which team has the most points in a single Premier League season?

c) Manchester City

Q31: Who won the Premier League title in the 2016-2017 season?

c) Chelsea

Q32: Who has scored the fastest goal in Premier League history?

a) Shane Long

Q33: Which team has the most consecutive seasons in the Premier League?

a) Arsenal

Q34: Who won the Premier League title in the 2015-2016 season?

c) Leicester City

Q35: Who has won the most Premier League Golden Boot awards?

a) Alan Shearer

Q36: Who scored the most goals in a single Premier League season?

a) Alan Shearer

Q37: Who won the Premier League title in the 2014-2015 season?

c) Chelsea

Q38: Who is the youngest player to captain a team in the Premier League?

a) Jack Wilshere

Q39: Which team has won the fewest points in a single Premier League season?

a) Derby County

Q40: Who won the Premier League title in the 2013-2014 season?

Manchester City

Q41: Who is the oldest player to debut in the Premier League?

Brad Friedel

Q42: Which team has the most goals in Premier League history?

Manchester United

Q43: Who won the Premier League title in the 2012-2013 season?

Manchester United

Q44: Who is the player with the most assists in a single Premier League season?

Kevin De Bruyne

Q45: Who is the all-time leading scorer in the Premier League?

Alan Shearer

Q46: Which club is known as the "Invincibles" after an unbeaten season?

Arsenal FC

Q47: Who holds the record for the most consecutive Premier League appearances?

Brad Friedel

Q48: Which Premier League team has the most consecutive wins in a single season?

Manchester City

Q49: Which player is often referred to as "Captain Fantastic" and played for Liverpool?

Steven Gerrard

Q50: Who is the youngest player to score a Premier League goal?

James Vaughan

Q51: Which Premier League club is known for its "You'll Never Walk Alone" anthem?

Liverpool FC

52: Which stadium has the record attendance for a Premier League match?

Old Trafford

Q53: Who is the player with the most Premier League appearances?

Gareth Barry

Q54: Which team won the Premier League title in the 2015/16 season against all odds?

Leicester City

Q55: Who is known as "The Special One" and has managed several Premier League clubs?

José Mourinho

Q56: Which Premier League club is often referred to as "The Red Devils"?

Manchester United

Q57: Which club's supporters are known as "The Kop"?

Liverpool FC

Q58: Who won the Premier League title in the 2019/20 season?

Liverpool FC

Q59: Which club has the nickname "The Gunners"?

Arsenal FC

Q60: Who holds the record for the most goals scored in a single Premier League season?

Alan Shearer

Q61: Which team has won the most consecutive Premier League titles?

c) Both

Q62: Who is the youngest player to make a Premier League appearance?

a) Harvey Elliott

Q63: Which club's supporters are known as "The Citizens"?

a) Manchester City FC

Q64: Who holds the record for the most consecutive Premier League clean sheets?

a) Petr Čech

Q65: Which club's supporters are known as "The Blues"?

a) Chelsea FC

Q66: Which club's supporters are known as "The Spurs"?

a) Tottenham Hotspur FC

Q67: Who holds the record for the most Premier League goals in

a calendar year?

a) Harry Kane

Q68: Who is the player with the most goals scored as a substitute in

Premier League history?

a) Jermain Defoe

Q69: Which club's supporters are known as "The Toffees"?

a) Everton FC

Q70: Who is the player with the most red cards in Premier League history?

a) Richard Dunne

Q71: Which club's supporters are known as "The Clarets"?

a) Burnley FC

Q72: Who is the player with the most own goals in Premier League history?

a) Richard Dunne

Q73: Which club's supporters are known as "The Canaries"?

a) Norwich City FC

Q74: Who is the player with the most Premier League appearances as a goalkeeper?

a) Petr Čech

Q75: Which team holds the record for the most consecutive away wins in the Premier League?

a) Chelsea FC

Q76: Which club's supporters are known as "The Hornets"?

a) Watford FC

Q77: Who is the player with the most Premier League hat-tricks?

a) Alan Shearer

Q78: Which team holds the record for the most consecutive Premier League draws?

a) Derby County

Q79: Which club's supporters are known as "The Baggies"?

a) West Bromwich Albion FC

Q80: Which club's supporters are known as "The Saints"?

a) Southampton FC

Q81: Which club's supporters are known as "The Eagles"?

a) Crystal Palace FC

Fa Cup

Q1: What is the FA Cup?

a) An annual knockout football competition in men's domestic English football

b) A biennial international football tournament

c) A regional football league in England

Q2: When was the first FA Cup held?

a) 1850-1851 season

b) 1871-1872 season

c) 1900-1901 season

Q3: Which team won the first FA Cup?

a) Manchester United

b) Wanderers FC

c) Liverpool FC

Q4: What is the format of the FA Cup?

a) Round-robin league format

b) Double elimination bracket

c) Knockout competition

Q5: Who has won the most FA Cup titles?

a) Manchester City

b) Arsenal

c) Chelsea

Q6: Which manager has won the most FA Cup titles?

a) Sir Alex Ferguson

b) Arsène Wenger

c) Jose Mourinho

Q7: When and where are the FA Cup semi-finals and final held?

a) Old Trafford

b) Anfield

c) Wembley Stadium

Q8: Who won the FA Cup 2022/23?

a) Manchester United

b) Manchester City

c) Liverpool FC

Q9: Who is the oldest club to have won the FA Cup?

a) Everton FC

b) Wanderers FC

c) Aston Villa

Q10: What is the record for the most goals scored by a player in a single FA Cup season?

a) 20 goals

b) 25 goals

c) 30 goals

Q11: What is the record for the most goals scored by a team in an FA Cup final?

a) 6 goals

b) 7 goals

c) 9 goals

Q12: Who scored the fastest goal in an FA Cup final?

a) Thierry Henry

b) Roberto Di Matteo

c) Alan Shearer

Q13: Which team holds the record for the highest FA Cup final victory?

a) Manchester United

b) Arsenal

c) Bury

Q14: Which team has won the most consecutive FA Cup titles?

a) Liverpool FC

b) Manchester City

c) Blackburn Rovers

Q15: Who is the all-time leading scorer in FA Cup history?

a) Wayne Rooney

b) Ian Rush

c) Alan Shearer

Q16: Who scored the most goals in a single FA Cup final?

a) Stan Mortensen

b) Didier Drogba

c) Cristiano Ronaldo

Q17: Which team has reached the most FA Cup finals without winning?

a) Everton FC

b) Tottenham Hotspur

c) Leicester City

Q18: Who is the player with the most FA Cup final appearances?

a) Ryan Giggs

b) Ashley Cole

c) Frank Lampard

Q19: Which team holds the record for the most FA Cup wins in a single decade?

a) Manchester United

b) Chelsea

c) Arsenal

Q20: Who scored the most goals in the total FA Cup finals?

a) Thierry Henry

b) Didier Drogba

c) Wayne Rooney

Q21: Which team has won the FA Cup the most times in a row?

a) Wanderers FC

b) Arsenal

c) Manchester United

Q22: Who is the only player to have scored a hat-trick in an FA Cup final?

a) Thierry Henry

b) Stan Mortensen

c) Geoff Hurst

Q23: Who is the player with the most assists in FA Cup history?

a) David Beckham

b) Steven Gerrard

c) Ryan Giggs

Q24: Which team has reached the most FA Cup finals?

a) Manchester United

b) Arsenal

c) Chelsea

Q25: Who is the only player to have scored in five different FA Cup finals?

a) Frank Lampard

b) Steven Gerrard

c) Didier Drogba

Q26: Which team won the FA Cup final with the highest aggregate score?

a) Arsenal

b) Manchester United

c) Blackpool

Q27: Which team won the longest FA Cup final replay?

a) Nottingham Forest

b) Sheffield United

c) Newcastle United

Q28: Which team has won the FA Cup the most times as a non-league club?

a) Tottenham Hotspur

b) Wimbledon

c) Wigan Athletic

Q29: Who is the player with the most goals in the FA Cup quarterfinals?

a) Thierry Henry

b) Ian Rush

c) Alan Shearer

Q30: Which team won the FA Cup final with the fewest goals scored

by both teams?

a) Bury

b) Derby County

c) Bolton Wanderers

Answers

Q1: What is the FA Cup?

a) An annual knockout football competition in men's domestic English football

Q2: When was the first FA Cup held?

b) 1871-1872 season

Q3: Which team won the first FA Cup?

b) Wanderers FC

Q4: What is the format of the FA Cup?

c) Knockout competition

Q5: Who has won the most FA Cup titles?

b) Arsenal

Q6: Which manager has won the most FA Cup titles?

a) Sir Alex Ferguson

Q7: When and where are the FA Cup semi-finals and final held?

c) Wembley Stadium

Q8: Who won the FA Cup 2022/23?

b) Manchester City

Q9: Who is the oldest club to have won the FA Cup?

b) Wanderers FC

Q10: What is the record for the most goals scored by a player in a single

FA Cup season?

c) 30 goals

Q11: What is the record for the most goals scored by a team in an FA

Cup final?

c) 9 goals

Q12: Who scored the fastest goal in an FA Cup final?

b) Roberto Di Matteo

Q13: Which team holds the record for the highest FA Cup final victory?

c) Bury

Q14: Which team has won the most consecutive FA Cup titles?

c) Blackburn Rovers

Q15: Who is the all-time leading scorer in FA Cup history?

b) Ian Rush

Q16: Who scored the most goals in a single FA Cup final?

a) Stan Mortensen

Q17: Which team has reached the most FA Cup finals without winning?

c) Leicester City

Q18: Who is the player with the most FA Cup final appearances?

b) Ashley Cole

Q19: Which team holds the record for the most FA Cup wins in a single decade?

a) Manchester United

Q20: Who scored the most goals in the total FA Cup finals?

b) Didier Drogba

Q21: Which team has won the FA Cup the most times in a row?

a) Wanderers FC

Q22: Who is the only player to have scored a hat-trick in an FA Cup final?

c) Geoff Hurst

Q23: Who is the player with the most assists in FA Cup history?

c) Ryan Giggs

Q24: Which team has reached the most FA Cup finals?

b) Arsenal

Q25: Who is the only player to have scored in five different FA Cup finals?

c) Didier Drogba

Q26: Which team won the FA Cup final with the highest aggregate score?

c) Blackpool

Q27: Which team won the longest FA Cup final replay?

a) Nottingham Forest

Q28: Which team has won the FA Cup the most times as a non-league club?

b) Wimbledon

Q29: Who is the player with the most goals in the FA Cup quarterfinals?

a) Thierry Henry

Q30: Which team won the FA Cup final with the fewest goals scored by

both teams?

b) Derby County

Champions League

Q1: What is the Champions League?

a) Europe's premier club football tournament organized by UEFA.

b) An international football club competition organized by FIFA.

Q2: When does the Champions League take place?

a) From January to October.

b) From April to November.

c) Annually from September to June.

Q3: How many teams participate in the Champions League?

a) 32 teams

b) 64 teams

c) 78 teams from 53 associations

Q4: How many teams compete in the group stage of the Champions League?

a) 8 teams

b) 16 teams

c) 32 teams competing for 16 places

Q5: Who won the Champions League in the 2022/2023 season?

a) Barcelona FC

b) Bayern Munich

c) Manchester City

Q6: Who was awarded the title of the best manager in the UEFA Champions League for the 2022/23 season?

a) Jurgen Klopp

b) Pep Guardiola

c) Zinedine Zidane

Q7: Who was the top scorer of the 2022/2023 Champions League season?

a) Lionel Messi

b) Cristiano Ronaldo

c) Erling Haaland

Q8: Who was named the best player of the 2022/2023 Champions League season?

a) Kevin De Bruyne

b) Rodri

c) Kylian Mbappe

Q9: How many matches were played in the 2022/2023 Champions League season?

a) 87 matches

b) 103 matches

c) 125 matches

Q10: What is the format of the Champions League?

a) Single-elimination tournament

b) Group stage followed by a knockout phase

c) Round-robin tournament

Q11: When was the first UEFA Champions League season held?

a) 1950-1951

b) 1960-1961

c) 1955-1956

Q12: Which club has won the most UEFA Champions League titles?

a) Liverpool FC

b) AC Milan

c) Real Madrid

Q13: Which player has won the most Champions League titles and how many?

a) Cristiano Ronaldo - 7 titles

b) Lionel Messi - 6 titles

c) Francisco Gento - 6 titles

Q14: Which club has the most appearances in the Champions League final and how many?

a) Manchester United - 14 times

b) Barcelona FC - 11 times

c) Real Madrid - 17 times

Q15: Who is the all-time leading scorer in the UEFA Champions League?

a) Thierry Henry

b) Raul

c) Cristiano Ronaldo

Q16: Who is the manager with the most UEFA Champions League titles?

a) Sir Alex Ferguson

b) Pep Guardiola

c) Zinedine Zidane

Q17: Who has won the most UEFA Champions League Golden Boot awards?

a) Robert Lewandowski

b) Lionel Messi

c) Cristiano Ronaldo

Q18: Who scored the fastest goal in a UEFA Champions League final?

a) Steven Gerrard

b) Paolo Maldini

c) Fernando Torres

Q19: Which team has won the UEFA Champions League three times

in a row?

a) FC Barcelona

b) Bayern Munich

c) Real Madrid

Q20: Who is the youngest player to score in a UEFA Champions League final?

a) Kylian Mbappe

b) Patrick Kluivert

c) Lionel Messi

Q21: Which club has won the most consecutive matches in a single UEFA Champions League season?

a) Bayern Munich

b) Real Madrid

c) Manchester City

Q22: Who is the player with the most assists in UEFA Champions League history?

a) Xavi Hernandez

b) Lionel Messi

c) Cristiano Ronaldo

Q23: Who holds the record for the most goals scored in a single UEFA Champions League season?

a) Lionel Messi

b) Cristiano Ronaldo

c) Robert Lewandowski

Q24: Which team holds the record for the highest number of goals in a single UEFA Champions League season?

a) FC Barcelona

b) Real Madrid

c) Bayern Munich

Q25: Who is the player with the most appearances in UEFA Champions League matches?

a) Ryan Giggs

b) Cristiano Ronaldo

c) Paolo Maldini

Q26: Which team has won the UEFA Champions League title the most times without losing a final?

a) AC Milan

b) Liverpool FC

c) Bayern Munich

Q27: Who is the only player to have won the UEFA Champions League with three different clubs?

a) Clarence Seedorf

b) Zlatan Ibrahimovic

c) Andrés Iniesta

Q28: Which club has the record for the most consecutive clean sheets in a single UEFA Champions League season?

a) Manchester United

b) FC Barcelona

c) Arsenal

Q29: Who is the player with the most assists in a single UEFA Champions League season?

a) Neymar

b) Kevin De Bruyne

c) Thomas Müller

Q30: Which club has won the UEFA Champions League title the most times without winning it consecutively?

a) AC Milan

b) Bayern Munich

c) FC Barcelona

Q31: Who is the only player to have scored in the final for two different winning teams?

a) Cristiano Ronaldo

b) Neymar

c) Zinedine Zidane

Q32: Which club has reached the most UEFA Champions League finals without winning the title?

a) Atletico Madrid

b) Juventus

c) AS Monaco

Q33: Who is the youngest player to captain a team in a UEFA Champions League final?

a) Iker Casillas

b) Steven Gerrard

c) Raúl

Q34: Which club has won the UEFA Champions League title the most times in a row?

a) Bayern Munich

b) Real Madrid

c) FC Barcelona

Q35: Who is the player with the most goals in UEFA Champions League knockout stage matches?

a) Cristiano Ronaldo

b) Lionel Messi

c) Robert Lewandowski

Q36: Which club has the record for the most consecutive appearances in

the UEFA Champions League?

a) Real Madrid

b) Bayern Munich

c) FC Barcelona

Q37: Who is the player with the most goals in UEFA Champions' League group stage matches?

a) Cristiano Ronaldo

b) Lionel Messi

c) Robert Lewandowski

Q38: Which club has the record for the highest aggregate score in a UEFA Champions League knockout tie?

a) FC Barcelona

b) Bayern Munich

c) Real Madrid

Q39: Who is the player with the most goals in UEFA Champions

League finals?

a) Cristiano Ronaldo

b) Lionel Messi

c) Raúl

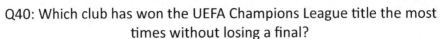

Q40: Which club has won the UEFA Champions League title the most times without losing a final?

a) AC Milan

b) Liverpool FC

c) Manchester United

Q41: Who is the player with the most assists in UEFA Champions League knockout stage matches?

a) Lionel Messi

b) Kevin De Bruyne

c) Xavi Hernandez

Q42: Which club has the record for the most goals in a single UEFA Champions League campaign?

a) Real Madrid

b) FC Barcelona

c) Bayern Munich

Q43: Who is the only player to have scored in the final for three different winning teams?

a) Cristiano Ronaldo

b) Lionel Messi

c) Zlatan Ibrahimovic

Q44: Who is the player with the most goals in the UEFA Champions League semifinals?

a) Cristiano Ronaldo

b) Lionel Messi

c) Robert Lewandowski

Q45: Which club has the record for the most goals in a single UEFA Champions League group-stage campaign?

a) Paris Saint-Germain

b) Bayern Munich

c) FC Barcelona

Q46: Who is the only player to have scored in the final for two different losing teams?

a) Arjen Robben

b) Gareth Bale

c) Steven Gerrard

Q47: Which club has reached the most UEFA Champions League finals without winning the title consecutively?

a) Liverpool FC

b) Bayern Munich

c) Juventus

Q48: Which club has reached the most UEFA Champions League semifinals?

a) Real Madrid

b) Bayern Munich

c) FC Barcelona

Q49: Who is the only player to have won the UEFA Champions League with three different clubs consecutively?

a) Clarence Seedorf

b) Cristiano Ronaldo

c) Xabi Alonso

Q50: Which club has the record for the most goals in a single UEFA Champions League quarterfinal tie?

a) FC Barcelona

b) Bayern Munich

c) Manchester United

Q51: Which club has the record for the highest aggregate score in a UEFA Champions League final?

a) Real Madrid

b) FC Barcelona

c) AC Milan

Q52: Who is the only player to have scored a hat-trick in a UEFA Champions League final?

a) Cristiano Ronaldo

b) Lionel Messi

c) Gareth Bale

Q53: Which club has reached the most consecutive UEFA Champions League quarterfinals?

a) FC Barcelona

b) Bayern Munich

c) Real Madrid

Q54: Who is the player with the most assists in UEFA Champions League group stage matches in a single season?

a) Neymar

b) Kevin De Bruyne

c) M.Salah

Answers

Q1: What is the Champions League?

a) Europe's premier club football tournament organized by UEFA.

Q2: When does the Champions League take place?

c) Annually from September to June.

Q3: How many teams participate in the Champions League?

c) 78 teams from 53 associations

Q4: How many teams compete in the group stage of the Champions League?

c) 32 teams competing for 16 places

Q5: Who won the Champions League in the 2022/2023 season?

c) Manchester City

Q6: Who was awarded the title of the best manager in the UEFA Champions League for the 2022/23 season?

b) Pep Guardiola

Q7: Who was the top scorer of the 2022/2023 Champions League season?

c) Erling Haaland

Q8: Who was named the best player of the 2022/2023 Champions League season?

b) Rodri

Q9: How many matches were played in the 2022/2023 Champions League season?

c) 125 matches

Q10: What is the format of the Champions League?

b) Group stage followed by a knockout phase

Q11: When was the first UEFA Champions League season held?

c) 1955-1956

Q12: Which club has won the most UEFA Champions League titles?

c) Real Madrid

Q13: Which player has won the most Champions League titles and how many?

c) Francisco Gento - 6 titles

Q14: Which club has the most appearances in the Champions League final and how many?

c) Real Madrid - 17 times

Q15: Who is the all-time leading scorer in the UEFA Champions League?

c) Cristiano Ronaldo

Q16: Who is the manager with the most UEFA Champions League titles?

c) Zinedine Zidane

Q17: Who has won the most UEFA Champions League Golden Boot awards?

c) Cristiano Ronaldo

Q18: Who scored the fastest goal in a UEFA Champions League final?

b) Paolo Maldini

Q19: Which team has won the UEFA Champions League three times in a row?

c) Real Madrid

Q20: Who is the youngest player to score in a UEFA Champions League final?

b) Patrick Kluivert

Q21: Which club has won the most consecutive matches in a single UEFA Champions League season?

a) Bayern Munich

Q22: Who is the player with the most assists in UEFA Champions League history?

a) Xavi Hernandez

Q23: Who holds the record for the most goals scored in a single UEFA Champions League season?

c) Cristiano Ronaldo

Q24: Which team holds the record for the highest number of goals in a single UEFA Champions League season?

b) Barcelona

Q25: Who is the player with the most appearances in UEFA Champions League matches?

b) Cristiano Ronaldo

Q26: Which team has won the UEFA Champions League title the most times without losing a final?

b) Liverpool FC

Q27: Who is the only player to have won the UEFA Champions League with three different clubs?

a) Clarence Seedorf

Q28: Which club has the record for the most consecutive clean sheets in a single UEFA Champions League season?

c) Arsenal

Q29: Who is the player with the most assists in a single UEFA Champions League season?

a) Neymar

Q30: Which club has won the UEFA Champions League title the most times without winning it consecutively?

c) FC Barcelona

Q31: Who is the only player to have scored in the final for two different winning teams?

c) Cristiano Ronaldo

Q32: Which club has reached the most UEFA Champions League finals without winning the title?

b) Juventus

Q33: Who is the youngest player to captain a team in a UEFA Champions League final?

b) Raúl

Q34: Which club has won the UEFA Champions League title the most times in a row?

a) Real Madrid

Q35: Who is the player with the most goals in UEFA Champions League knockout stage matches?

a) Cristiano Ronaldo

Q36: Which club has the record for the most consecutive appearances in the UEFA Champions League?

b) Real Madrid

Q37: Who is the player with the most goals in UEFA Champions League group stage matches?

b) Lionel Messi

Q38: Which club has the record for the highest aggregate score in a UEFA Champions League knockout tie?

c) Bayern Munich

Q39: Who is the player with the most goals in UEFA Champions League finals?

a) Cristiano Ronaldo

Q40: Which club has won the UEFA Champions League title the most times without losing a final?

b) AC Milan

Q41: Who is the player with the most assists in UEFA Champions League knockout stage matches?

a) Lionel Messi

Q42: Which club has the record for the most goals in a single UEFA Champions League campaign?

b) FC Barcelona

Q43: Who is the only player to have scored in the final for three different winning teams?

a) Cristiano Ronaldo

Q44: Who is the player with the most goals in the UEFA Champions League semifinals?

a) Cristiano Ronaldo

Q45: Which club has the record for the most goals in a single UEFA Champions League group-stage campaign?

a) Paris Saint-Germain

Q46: Who is the only player to have scored in the final for two different

losing teams?

a) Arjen Robben

Q47: Which club has reached the most UEFA Champions League finals
without winning the title consecutively?

a) Liverpool FC

Q48: Which club has reached the most UEFA Champions League semifinals?

a) Real Madrid

Q49: Who is the only player to have won the UEFA Champions League with
three different clubs consecutively?

a) Clarence Seedorf

Q50: Which club has the record for the most goals in a single UEFA
Champions League quarterfinal tie?

a) Bayern Munich

Q51: Which club has the record for the highest aggregate score in a UEFA
Champions League final?

b) Real Madrid

Q52: Who is the only player to have scored a hat-trick in a UEFA Champions
League final?

a) Cristiano Ronaldo

Q53: Which club has reached the most consecutive UEFA Champions

League quarterfinals?

b) Bayern Munich

Q54: Who is the player with the most assists in UEFA Champions

League group stage matches in a single season?

a) Neymar

Europa League

Q1: Who was the champion of the tournament 2022/23?

a) Manchester City

b) Chelsea

c) Sevilla

Q2: Which player scored the most goals in the tournament in 2022/23?

a) Marcus Rashford

b) Victor Boniface

c) Erling Haaland

Q3: Who provided the most assists during the tournament 2022/23?

a) Evander

b) Kevin De Bruyne

c) Bruno Fernandes

Q4: Who kept the most clean sheets among goalkeepers in 2022/23?

a) Rui Patrício

b) Ederson

c) Thibaut Courtois

Q5: When was the first UEFA Europa League season held?

a) 1970-1971

b) 1971-1972

c) 1972-1973

Q6: Which club has won the most UEFA Europa League titles?

a) Sevilla FC

b) FC Porto

c) Juventus

Q7: Who is the all-time leading scorer in the UEFA Europa League?

a) Henrik Larsson

b) Radamel Falcao

c) Alan Shearer

Q8: Who is the manager with the most UEFA Europa League titles?

a) Unai Emery

b) Giovanni Trapattoni

c) Jürgen Klopp

Q9: Who has won the most UEFA Europa League Golden Boot awards?

a) Radamel Falcao

b) Klaas-Jan Huntelaar

c) Pierre-Emerick Aubameyang

Q10: Who scored the fastest goal in a UEFA Europa League final?

a) Jesús Navas

b) Diego Forlán

c) Henrik Larsson

Q11: Which team has won the UEFA Europa League three times in a row?

a) Sevilla FC

b) Atletico Madrid

c) FC Porto

Q12: Who is the youngest player to score in a UEFA Europa League final?

a) Branislav Ivanović

b) Kylian Mbappé

c) Erling Haaland

Q13: Which club has won the UEFA Europa League title the most times without losing a final?

a) Sevilla FC

b) AC Milan

c) Atletico Madrid

Q14: Who is the only player to have won the UEFA Europa League with three different clubs?

a) Raphaël Varane

b) Fernando Torres

c) Sergio Ramos

Q15: Who holds the record for the most goals scored in a single UEFA Europa League season?

a) Radamel Falcao

b) Klaas-Jan Huntelaar

c) Aritz Aduriz

Q16: Which team holds the record for the highest number of goals in a single UEFA Europa League season?

a) FC Porto

b) Sevilla FC

c) Atletico Madrid

Q17: Who is the player with the most appearances in UEFA Europa League matches?

a) Giuseppe Bergomi

b) Zlatan Ibrahimovic

c) Steven Gerrard

Q18: Who is the player with the most goals scored in UEFA Europa League knockout stage matches?

a) Radamel Falcao

b) Olivier Giroud

c) Alan Shearer

Q19: Which team holds the record for the most consecutive appearances in the UEFA Europa League?

a) FC Salzburg

b) Sevilla FC

c) AC Milan

Q20: Who is the player with the most assists in UEFA Europa League history?

a) Ever Banega

b) Mesut Özil

c) Cesc Fàbregas

Q21: Which team holds the record for the most consecutive clean sheets in a single UEFA Europa League season?

a) Atalanta

b) Manchester United

c) AC Milan

Q22: Who is the player with the most assists in a single UEFA Europa League season?

a) Henrikh Mkhitaryan

b) Mesut Özil

c) Bruno Fernandes

Q23: Which club has won the UEFA Europa League title the most times without winning it consecutively?

a) Atlético Madrid

b) FC Sevilla

c) Chelsea

Q24: Who is the only player to have scored in the final for two different winning teams?

a) Dmitri Alenichev

b) Cristiano Ronaldo

c) Lionel Messi

Q25: Which club has reached the most UEFA Europa League finals without winning the title?

a) SL Benfica

b) Tottenham Hotspur

c) Napoli

Q26: Which team holds the record for the most goals in a single UEFA Europa League group-stage campaign?

a) FC Salzburg

b) Arsenal

c) Borussia Dortmund

Q27: Who is the only player to have scored in the final for two different losing teams?

a) Dmitri Alenichev

b) Arjen Robben

c) Didier Drogba

Q28: Which team holds the record for the most goals in a single UEFA Europa League knockout tie?

a) FC Porto

b) Liverpool FC

c) AC Milan

Q29: Who is the only player to have won the UEFA Europa League with three different clubs and scored in the final for each?

a) Fernando Torres

b) Zlatan Ibrahimovic

c) Andrés Iniesta

Q30: Which team holds the record for the highest aggregate score in a UEFA Europa League final?

a) Atlético Madrid

b) FC Sevilla

c) Chelsea

Answers

Q1: Who was the champion of the tournament 2022/23?

c) Sevilla

Q2: Which player scored the most goals in the tournament in 2022/23?

a) Marcus Rashford

Q3: Who provided the most assists during the tournament 2022/23?

a) Evander

Q4: Who kept the most clean sheets among goalkeepers in 2022/23?

a) Rui Patrício

Q5: When was the first UEFA Europa League season held?

b) 1971-1972

Q6: Which club has won the most UEFA Europa League titles?

a) Sevilla FC

Q7: Who is the all-time leading scorer in the UEFA Europa League?

a) Henrik Larsson

Q8: Who is the manager with the most UEFA Europa League titles?

a) Unai Emery

Q9: Who has won the most UEFA Europa League Golden Boot awards?

a) Radamel Falcao

Q10: Who scored the fastest goal in a UEFA Europa League final?

a) Jesús Navas

Q11: Which team has won the UEFA Europa League three times in a row?

a) Sevilla FC

Q12: Who is the youngest player to score in a UEFA Europa League final?

a) Branislav Ivanović

Q13: Which club has won the UEFA Europa League title the most times without losing a final?

a) Sevilla FC

Q14: Who is the only player to have won the UEFA Europa League with three different clubs?

a) Raphaël Varane

Q15: Who holds the record for the most goals scored in a single UEFA Europa League season?

a) Radamel Falcao

Q16: Which team holds the record for the highest number of goals in a single UEFA Europa League season?

b) Sevilla FC

Q17: Who is the player with the most appearances in UEFA Europa League matches?

a) Giuseppe Bergomi

Q18: Who is the player with the most goals scored in UEFA Europa League knockout stage matches?

a) Radamel Falcao

Q19: Which team holds the record for the most consecutive appearances in the UEFA Europa League?

a) FC Salzburg

Q20: Who is the player with the most assists in UEFA Europa League history?

a) Ever Banega

Q21: Which team holds the record for the most consecutive clean sheets in a single UEFA Europa League season?

a) Atalanta

Q22: Who is the player with the most assists in a single UEFA Europa League season?

a) Henrikh Mkhitaryan

Q23: Which club has won the UEFA Europa League title the most times without winning it consecutively?

a) Atlético Madrid

Q24: Who is the only player to have scored in the final for two different winning teams?

a) Dmitri Alenichev

Q25: Which club has reached the most UEFA Europa League finals without winning the title?

a) SL Benfica

Q26: Which team holds the record for the most goals in a single UEFA Europa League group-stage campaign?

a) FC Salzburg

Q27: Who is the only player to have scored in the final for two different losing teams?

a) Dmitri Alenichev

Q28: Which team holds the record for the most goals in a single UEFA Europa League knockout tie?

a) FC Porto

Q29: Who is the only player to have won the UEFA Europa League with three different clubs and scored in the final for each?

a) Fernando Torres

Q30: Which team holds the record for the highest aggregate score in a UEFA Europa League final?

a) Atlético Madrid

La Liga

Q1: When was the first La Liga season held?

a) 1929

b) 1935

c) 1942

Q2: Which club has won the most La Liga titles?

a) Real Madrid

b) Barcelona

c) Atlético Madrid

Q3: Who won the La Liga 2022/23?

a) Barcelona

b) Real Madrid

c) Sevilla

Q4: Who was the top scorer of the La Liga 2022/23 season?

a) Lionel Messi

b) Karim Benzema

c) Robert Lewandowski

Q5: Who were the top assists of the La Liga 2022/23 season?

a) Lionel Messi

b) ANTOINE GRIEZMANN

c) Dani Olmo

Q6: Who is the all-time leading scorer in La Liga?

a) Lionel Messi

b) Cristiano Ronaldo

c) Telmo Zarra

Q7: Who holds the record for the most goals in a single La Liga season?

a) Lionel Messi

b) Cristiano Ronaldo

c) Telmo Zarra

Q8: Which club holds the record for the longest unbeaten streak in La Liga?

a) Real Madrid

b) Barcelona

c) Real Sociedad

Q9: Who is the player with the most assists in La Liga history?

a) Lionel Messi

b) Xavi

c) Andrés Iniesta

Q10: Which team holds the record for the most goals scored in a single La Liga season?

a) FC Barcelona

b) Real Madrid

c) Atletico Madrid

Q11: Who is the manager with the most La Liga titles?

a) Miguel Muñoz

b) Carlo Ancelotti

c) Zinedine Zidane

Q12: Who is the youngest player to score in a La Liga match?

a) Fabrice Olinga

b) Ansu Fati

c) Bojan Krkic

Q13: Which club has the longest consecutive streak of La Liga titles?

a) Real Madrid

b) Barcelona

c) Atlético Madrid

Q14: Who is the player with the most appearances in La Liga matches?

a) Andoni Zubizarreta

b) Sergio Ramos

c) Lionel Messi

Q15: Which club holds the record for the most consecutive La Liga wins?

a) FC Barcelona

b) Real Madrid

c) Atlético Madrid

Q16: Who is the player with the most hat tricks in La Liga history?

a) Lionel Messi

b) Cristiano Ronaldo

c) Telmo Zarra

Q17: Which club holds the record for the most consecutive La Liga matches without conceding a goal?

a) FC Barcelona

b) Real Madrid

c) Atlético Madrid

Q18: Who is the player with the most La Liga titles?

a) Paco Gento

b) Xavi Hernandez

c) Andrés Iniesta

Q19: Which club holds the record for the most consecutive La Liga seasons without relegation?

a) FC Barcelona

b) Real Madrid

c) Athletic Bilbao

Q20: Who is the player with the most La Liga assists in a single season?

a) Xavi Hernandez

b) Lionel Messi

c) Dani Carvajal

Q21: Which club holds the record for the most points earned in a single La Liga season?

a) FC Barcelona

b) Real Madrid

c) Atlético Madrid

Q22: Who is the youngest La Liga top scorer?

a) Lionel Messi

b) Karim Benzema

c) Ansu Fati

Q23: Which club holds the record for the highest goal difference in a single La Liga season?

a) Real Madrid

b) FC Barcelona

c) Atlético Madrid

Q24: Who is the player with the most consecutive La Liga appearances?

a) Sergio Ramos

b) Lionel Messi

c) Xavi Hernandez

Q25: Which club holds the record for the most consecutive seasons in La Liga?

a) Real Madrid

b) FC Barcelona

c) Athletic Bilbao

Q26: Who is the player with the most La Liga assists in a career?

a) Lionel Messi

b) Xavi Hernandez

c) Andrés Iniesta

Q27: Which club holds the record for the most La Liga titles in a row?

a) FC Barcelona

b) Real Madrid

c) Atlético Madrid

Q28: Who is the player with the most La Liga hat-tricks?

a) Lionel Messi

b) Cristiano Ronaldo

c) Telmo Zarra

Q29: Which club holds the record for the most La Liga goals in a single season?

a) FC Barcelona

b) Real Madrid

c) Atlético Madrid

Q30: Which club holds the record for the most La Liga away wins in a single season?

a) Real Madrid

b) FC Barcelona

c) Valencia CF

Q31: Who is the player with the most La Liga goals in El Clásico matches?

a) Lionel Messi

b) Cristiano Ronaldo

c) Alfredo Di Stéfano

Q32: Who is the player with the most goals from direct free-kicks in La Liga?

a) Lionel Messi

b) Cristiano Ronaldo

c) Ronald Koeman

Q33: Which club holds the record for the most consecutive La Liga home victories?

a) FC Barcelona

b) Real Madrid

c) Sevilla FC

Q34: Who is the player with the most La Liga goals from penalties?

a) Cristiano Ronaldo

b) Lionel Messi

c) Hugo Sánchez

Q35: Which club holds the record for the most goals scored in La Liga history?

a) Real Madrid

b) FC Barcelona

c) Atlético Madrid

Q36: Who is the player with the most La Liga goals from outside the penalty area?

a) Lionel Messi

b) Cristiano Ronaldo

c) David Beckham

Q37: Who is the player with the most La Liga goals scored in one calendar year?

a) Lionel Messi

b) Cristiano Ronaldo

c) Telmo Zarra

Q38: Who is the player with the most La Liga assists in El Clásico matches?

a) Lionel Messi

b) Xavi Hernandez

c) Luis Figo

Q39: Who is the player with the most La Liga goals from headers?

a) Cristiano Ronaldo

b) Fernando Llorente

c) Aritz Aduriz

Q40: Who is the player with the most La Liga assists from set-pieces?

a) Lionel Messi

b) Xavi Hernandez

c) David Beckham

Answers

Q1: When was the first La Liga season held?

a) 1929

Q2: Which club has won the most La Liga titles?

a) Real Madrid

Q3: Who won the La Liga 2022/23?

a) Barcelona

Q4: Who was the top scorer of the La Liga 2022/23 season?

a) Robert Lewandowski

Q5: Who were the top assists of the La Liga 2022/23 season?

a) ANTOINE GRIEZMANN

Q6: Who is the all-time leading scorer in La Liga?

a) Lionel Messi

Q7: Who holds the record for the most goals in a single La Liga season?

a) Lionel Messi

Q8: Which club holds the record for the longest unbeaten streak in La Liga?

a) Real Sociedad

Q9: Who is the player with the most assists in La Liga history?

a) Lionel Messi

Q10: Which team holds the record for the most goals scored in a single La Liga season?

a) FC Barcelona

Q11: Who is the manager with the most La Liga titles?

a) Miguel Muñoz

Q12: Who is the youngest player to score in a La Liga match?

a) Fabrice Olinga

Q13: Which club has the longest consecutive streak of La Liga titles?

a) Real Madrid

Q14: Who is the player with the most appearances in La Liga matches?

a) Andoni Zubizarreta

Q15: Which club holds the record for the most consecutive La Liga wins?

a) FC Barcelona

Q16: Who is the player with the most hat tricks in La Liga history?

a) Lionel Messi

Q17: Which club holds the record for the most consecutive La Liga matches without conceding a goal?

a) FC Barcelona

Q18: Who is the player with the most La Liga titles?

a) Paco Gento

Q19: Which club holds the record for the most consecutive La Liga seasons without relegation?

a) FC Barcelona

Q20: Who is the player with the most La Liga assists in a single season?

a) Xavi Hernandez

Q21: Which club holds the record for the most points earned in a single La Liga season?

a) FC Barcelona

Q22: Who is the youngest La Liga top scorer?

c) Ansu Fati

Q23: Which club holds the record for the highest goal difference in a single La Liga season?

a) Real Madrid

Q24: Who is the player with the most consecutive La Liga appearances?

a) Sergio Ramos

Q25: Which club holds the record for the most consecutive seasons in La Liga?

b) FC Barcelona

Q26: Who is the player with the most La Liga assists in a career?

b) Xavi Hernandez

Q27: Which club holds the record for the most La Liga titles in a row?

a) FC Barcelona

Q28: Who is the player with the most La Liga hat-tricks?

a) Lionel Messi

Q29: Which club holds the record for the most La Liga goals in a single season?

a) FC Barcelona

Q30: Which club holds the record for the most La Liga away wins in a single season?

a) Real Madrid

Q31: Who is the player with the most La Liga goals in El Clásico matches?

a) Lionel Messi

Q32: Who is the player with the most goals from direct free-kicks in La Liga?

a) Lionel Messi

Q33: Which club holds the record for the most consecutive La Liga home victories?

b) Real Madrid

Q34: Who is the player with the most La Liga goals from penalties?

a) Cristiano Ronaldo

Q35: Which club holds the record for the most goals scored in La Liga history?

a) Real Madrid

Q36: Who is the player with the most La Liga goals from outside the penalty area?

a) Lionel Messi

Q37: Who is the player with the most La Liga goals scored in one calendar year?

a) Lionel Messi

Q38: Who is the player with the most La Liga assists in El Clásico matches?

a) Lionel Messi

Q39: Who is the player with the most La Liga goals from headers?

b) Fernando Llorente

Q40: Who is the player with the most La Liga assists from set-pieces?

b) Xavi Hernandez

Seria A

Q1: Which team won the Serie A title in 2022/23?

a) Napoli

b) Lazio

c) Inter Milan

Q2: Which team finished as the runner-up in Serie A 2022/23?

a) Napoli

b) Lazio

c) Inter Milan

Q3: Which teams qualified for the UEFA Champions League from Serie A 2022/23?

a) Napoli and Lazio

b) Inter Milan and AC Milan

c) Napoli, Lazio, Inter Milan, and AC Milan

Q4: Which teams qualified for the UEFA Europa League from Serie A 2022/23?

a) Napoli and Lazio

b) Inter Milan and AC Milan

c) Atalanta and Roma

Q5: Who was the top scorer of Serie A 2022/23?

a) Victor Osimhen

b) Lorenzo Insigne

c) Ciro Immobile

Q6: Who was the best player of Serie A 2022/23?

a) Lorenzo Insigne

b) Ciro Immobile

c) Gianluigi Donnarumma

Q7: Who was the best goalkeeper of Serie A 2022/23?

a) Gianluigi Donnarumma

b) Wojciech Szczęsny

c) Samir Handanović

Q8: Which team has won the most Serie A titles?

a) Juventus

b) AC Milan

c) Inter Milan

Q9: Which team holds the record for most consecutive Serie A titles?

a) Juventus

b) AC Milan

c) Inter Milan

Q10: Which player has scored the most goals in Serie A history?

a) Silvio Piola

b) Francesco Totti

c) Gunnar Nordahl

Q11: Which player has scored the most goals in a single Serie A season?

a) Gonzalo Higuaín

b) Francesco Totti

c) Gabriel Batistuta

Q12: Which player has won the most Serie A Golden Boots, awarded to the top scorer of each season?

a) Paulo Dybala

b) Gunnar Nordahl

c) Alessandro Del Piero

Q13: Which player has won the most Serie A MVP awards, given to the best player of each season?

a) Paulo Dybala

b) Francesco Totti

c) Gianluigi Buffon

Q14: Which player has made the most appearances in Serie A history?

a) Paolo Maldini

b) Francesco Totti

c) Gianluigi Buffon

Q15: Which player has made the most consecutive appearances in Serie A history?

a) Gianluigi Buffon

b) Alessandro Del Piero

c) Francesco Totti

Q16: Which player has won the most Serie A titles as a captain?

a) Giuseppe Furino

b) Francesco Totti

c) Paolo Maldini

Q17: Which player has scored the most hat tricks in Serie A history?

a) Gunnar Nordahl

b) Giuseppe Meazza

c) Alessandro Del Piero

Q18: Which team has scored the most goals in Serie A history?

a) Juventus

b) AC Milan

c) Inter Milan

Q19: Which team has scored the most goals in a single Serie A season?

a) Torino

b) Napoli

c) Inter Milan

Q20: Which team has conceded the fewest goals in a single Serie A season?

a) Juventus

b) AC Milan

c) Inter Milan

Q21: Which team has the best goal difference in a single Serie A season?

a) Torino

b) Milan

c) Juventus

Q22: Which team has won the most matches in Serie A history?

a) Juventus

b) Milan

c) Inter Milan

Q23: Which team has won the most matches in a single Serie A season?

a) Juventus

b) Inter Milan

c) Milan

Q24: Which team has won the most home matches in a single Serie A season?

a) Juventus

b) Inter Milan

c) Milan

Q25: Which team has won the most away matches in a single Serie A season?

a) Milan

b) Juventus

c) Inter Milan

Q26: Which team has the longest unbeaten streak in Serie A history?

a) Milan

b) Juventus

c) Inter Milan

Q27: Which team has the most consecutive wins in Serie A history?

a) Inter Milan

b) Juventus

c) Milan

Q28: Which team has the most consecutive wins in a single Serie A season?

a) Roma

b) Juventus

c) Inter Milan

Q29: Which team has the most consecutive away wins in Serie A history?

a) Roma

b) Milan

c) Juventus

Q30: Which player has scored the most goals from penalties in Serie A history?a

a) Francesco Totti

b) Alessandro Del Piero

c) Roberto Baggio

Answers

Q1: Which team won the Serie A title in 2022/23?

a) Napoli

Q2: Which team finished as the runner-up in Serie A 2022/23?

b) Lazio

Q3: Which teams qualified for the UEFA Champions League from Serie A 2022/23?

c) Napoli, Lazio, Inter Milan, and AC Milan

Q4: Which teams qualified for the UEFA Europa League from Serie A 2022/23?

c) Atalanta and Roma

Q5: Who was the top scorer of Serie A 2022/23?

a) Victor Osimhen

Q6: Who was the best player of Serie A 2022/23?

a) Lorenzo Insigne

Q7: Who was the best goalkeeper of Serie A 2022/23?

a) Gianluigi Donnarumma

Q8: Which team has won the most Serie A titles?

a) Juventus

Q9: Which team holds the record for most consecutive Serie A titles?

a) Juventus

Q10: Which player has scored the most goals in Serie A history?

a) Silvio Piola

Q11: Which player has scored the most goals in a single Serie A season?

a) Gonzalo Higuaín

Q12: Which player has won the most Serie A Golden Boots?

b) Gunnar Nordahl

Q13: Which player has won the most Serie A MVP awards?

a) Paulo Dybala

Q14: Which player has made the most appearances in Serie A history?

a) Paolo Maldini

Q15: Which player has made the most consecutive appearances in Serie A history?

a) Gianluigi Buffon

Q16: Which player has won the most Serie A titles as a captain?

c) Paolo Maldini

Q17: Which player has scored the most hat tricks in Serie A history?

a) Gunnar Nordahl

Q18: Which team has scored the most goals in Serie A history?

a) Juventus

Q19: Which team has scored the most goals in a single Serie A season?

a) Torino

Q20: Which team has conceded the fewest goals in a single Serie A season?

a) Juventus

Q21: Which team has the best goal difference in a single Serie A season?

a) Torino

Q22: Which team has won the most matches in Serie A history?

a) Juventus

Q23: Which team has won the most matches in a single Serie A season?

a) Juventus

Q24: Which team has won the most home matches in a single Serie A season?

a) Juventus

Q25: Which team has won the most away matches in a single Serie A season?

a) Milan

Q26: Which team has the longest unbeaten streak in Serie A history?

a) Milan

Q27: Which team has the most consecutive wins in Serie A history?

a) Inter Milan

Q28: Which team has the most consecutive wins in a single Serie A season?

a) Roma

Q29: Which team has the most consecutive away wins in Serie A history?

a) Roma

Q30: Which player has scored the most goals from penalties in Serie A history?

a) Francesco Totti

Printed in Great Britain
by Amazon

32107940R00069